Love is for the Birds

Designed and published 2011 in Cork by
Onstream Publications, www.onstream.ie
© Marcia Wrixon

Typing from original manuscript by Gene and Barbara Courtney

ISBN: 978 1 897685 61 7

Printed in Ireland by KPS Colourprint

Love is for the Birds

by

MARCIA WRIXON

To Marcia
with lots and lots of love

and
in memory of Harold, whose idea this was

1 November 2011

Artwork

Paintings 4, 12, 18, 20, 26, 38   Shane Johnson
Paintings 6, 44   Marcia Wrixon
Photograph 17   Marcia Wrixon
Cover drawing and paintings 28, 36   Katherine Boucher Beug
Drawings 14, 30   Liam Kelly
Photographs 2, 42   Joachim Beug
Photograph 34   Alannah Hopkin
Back cover photograph   Mary Wrixon

Poems

La Perduta
Rome 2002

The city map whose twelve great routes misleading,
Towards monument of rulers, fast succeeding,
Beset by obelisks which point to glory,
Has plunged me into chiaroscuro light
A maze of streets which may be wrong or right.
I steal in Eamon's shadow as he marches
Lest I be lost beneath the many arches.
The lives of saints and pagan lore confusing
My notion of morality I'm losing.
In vapour died Cecelia chaste and good
Resilient Daphne turned herself to wood.
While Leda and Europa fell to Jove
And St Teresa knew angelic love.
No devil born in hell the arts pursuing,
At images I gaze while vaguely viewing
Archaic lines of poetry inscripted
Or ancient Latin cunningly encrypted.
A magister oracular I'm needing
Oh Damn, Alas, I see his back receding!

Confound the path from Rome to Amor,
The long way round is far the Grandest Tour.

The Highs and Lows of Venice
2003

The stones of Venezia yearning to fly,
Float on the water and blend with the sky.
A failure of gravitas, lacking in heft,
A circuitous city without right or left,
An identity crisis of virtue and sin
Of heavenly quiet and clamorous din,
Where virgin assumptions and carnival fun
Can mingle as freely as rainclouds and sun.
Miraculous churches and houses with curses,
Gondolas for lovers which double as hearses.
If lions could fly and if horses could climb,
We might understand if we travelled in time
The quirky persona who lives in these bricks
An ancient signora who knows a few tricks.
Is she outwardly faded with heart of pure gold?
Or artfully draped, but decrepit and old?
A Byzantine beauty with Renaissance dreams,
The only thing certain, she's not what she seems.

Another Year, Another Hat

for Joachim, December 2003
With thanks to Pauline Hall, and her list of rhyming hats

Time was, to be just 'comme il faut'
You had to wear the right chapeau.
The key to someone's true estate
Was in the hat upon his pate.
From peasant cap of subjugation
To crown of kingly elevation,
Rakish tilt of artist's beret
Jester's bells for making merry,
Deer stalker of the mountain hiker,
Helmet of the daring biker,
Veil and brim for angry bees,
Mitre to bring 'em to their knees.
Judges wig for mounting benches
Homburg to attract the wenches
Camouflage to hide in trenches
Sou'wester for the stormy drenches …
Imagine, then a bright cockade,
Saluting headgear on parade
Braided cap of brigadier
Ribboned hat of bandolier
Straw hat of the gondolier
Tricorne hat of buccaneer
Busby of the grenadier
Top hat of the financier
Fedora of the racketeer
Turban of the Grand Vizier …
Newer styles may yet appear,
But where are the hats of yesteryear?

Christmas 2003

On Christmas night did angels play electrical guitars?
Was manger hung with pulsing lights which blotted out the stars?

Was Mary wearing trendy gear ... all glitter style and glam?
Did shepherds dine on cakes and pies, on turkey, beef and ham?

Did Magi drink a welcome cup of spirit to the brim?
Then fall about with laughter, till their senses all went dim?

And what about the gifts they brought? Nike shoes and jackets?
Mobile phones and DVDs, and sweets in coloured packets?

Was Bethlehem decked out that night with tinsel bell and balls?
Did Bedouin ride camels to the nearest shopping malls?

What has happened to our night of holiness and peace,
The message of Salvation when all stress and strife should cease?

Men of good will, and women too, return unto your senses.
Let Love and Joy reclaim your hearts, and spare the great expenses.

Shell-Collecting

February 2004: Palm Beach, Florida

Crescent of beach that embraces the sea
Fogbound and spellbound, content just to be
Walking and gathering shells in the tide –
A whelk now abandoned, a hole in its side,
A mollusk's great mansion no longer a home,
Broken and damaged and left in the foam;
Wings of an angel; dollars of sand,
Collecting too much to retain in my hand.
Sea-battered corals from far-distant reef.
I bring them along in the hope, or belief,
That they may find a place on a table or shelf,
But I never regard them again, nor myself …
And the gleam that they had when they rolled in the tide
Faded and paled when at last home and dried.
The fragile constructions, the small works of art,
Their beauty gave rise to a calcified heart.
To live in the ocean no longer a goal.
Nor could I return to the deeps of my soul.

Memory
May 25, 2004

My memory of late seems to be very flawed
Or is it perhaps that it's just over-awed?
A staggering number of years to recall
I couldn't expect to remember them all!
The travels, the parties, the operas, the plays,
Can you give me the dates? or the months? or the days?
I don't know the name, and I don't know the face,
And I can't be too sure of the time or the place ...
And the things that I learned in my long-ago school,
When I try to recite them, I feel quite a fool.
I used to know chapter and verse off by heart,
But it's much more a case now of stop, than of start.
In the pool of oblivion once more I plunge
My hard-wired brain has the texture of sponge.
The arteries, synapses, dendrites go hard
While the lean meat of memory is turning to lard.
Make new connections? Use all that pith?
The megabyte mind is a faraway myth.
Drifting thru dreams and enveloped by haze
The pathway to reason is lost in a maze.
And all that I once was, and will be and am,
Amounts to a dubious download of spam!

Broadway

for 2004 on New Year's Eve

I love the bawdy nights
    The coloured lights
    The silky tights   of Broadway

    The latest news
    The public views
    The bad reviews   of Broadway

    The frumpy clowns
    The ups and downs
    The smiles and frowns   of Broadway

    The push and shove
    The hand in glove
    The lust and love   of Broadway

    The past her best
    The overdressed
    The treasure chest   of Broadway

    The farce and fun
    Extended run
    The smoking gun   of Broadway

    The on their feet
    The pulsing beat
    The dirty street   of Broadway

The song and dance
The backward glance
The doomed romance   of Broadway

The neon glare
The stop and stare
It's in the air   of Broadway

You're looking fine
Will you be mine?
The Auld Lang Syne   of Broadway

When time descends his silver chain
The old refrain
begins again,   on Broadway

After the Party
for Mary & Denis Wilson

Neath Eglantine's green leafy shade
Their tardy way the Wrixons made
Arriving to a welcome din …
The hostess came and let us in.
Drinks all round, and then the food
Fish and salads, very gooood.
The just desserts at last were served
When to the sitting room we swerved
And gave the best of song & verse
From 'excellent' to 'could be worse' …

Oriana's repertoire
Commented proceedings for the soir
She sang with style, she sang with flair
Piano ringing in the air
Gerry quickly took his cue
He gave us milkmaids, heifers too
His stock of pastoral delights
Could keep us up for several nights.
Then Paddy sang … a sterling note
Issued from his silver throat,
Then Betty offered childhood rhymes
Transporting us to olden times.
And Harold, not to be undone
Added anecdotal fun.
And Marcia, well, enough's been said,
I think it's time I went to bed.

I'll dwell in Marble Halls tonight
Lit by Mary's star so bright,
But not before I offer praise
To host and hostess for the ways
In which they entertained each guest
They gave their all, we did our best
And magically, or so it seems
The music echoes in my dreams.

13

Siena 9/5/05

14

Bacchanal

for the Uncorked Bottle Club
Sienna, May 2005

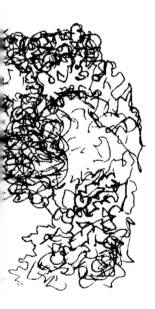

Charioted by the touring bus,
No other passengers – just us,
Driving through the creten clay,
Or winding hills, or motorway,
To tortured spread of canopy
Hiding purple panoply
Of grapes, whose nature will transmute,
Making spirit out of fruit,
To lie as ruby wine exalted
Deep within the tunnel vaulted
Reclining on a bed of dust
To meet the hand and corkscrew thrust
Of ribald rabelaisian males
Who drain again their glassy grails …
And sing beneath the crescent moon
Till daybreak comes a bit too soon.
Tomorrow they'll be heading home,
Passing through the streets of Rome,
Bearing booty, mouthing prayer
For weather fine and harvest fair,
Bringing from the barren fields
The miracle of future yields.

Per Teresa
Sandycove, June 2005

Parlando come studente
Abbiamo fatto niente.
Non abbiamo lavorato
Ma invece divorato
Tarte e biscotti
Alla casa cacciotti.

E forse la ragione
Perche questa staggione
Preferisce la piscine
All bella Terracina.

Una torre privata
Con bella climata
Ciama ai cuori
E guida li fiori
Dal isola alta.
Due difficile scelta!

Allora addio.
Diciamo con brio,
'Retorna qui presto!'
Pasare il resto
Della vita favolosa,
In baia sabbiosa.

A Bovine Comedy

For Richard on his birthday, December 2005

A Bovine Comedy, all eyes ears and horn
Seeks to attract attention
But eloquence belongs to the tree of thorn
Silent in its intention
To endure whatever situation
Eludes such rapt anticipation.
Mere meat and milk cannot outface
The evidence,
Gathered in this time and place:
Cow-incidence.

Swan Song

To the tune of 'One Day in Kilkenny I Called on Ms Brown'

Our host and our hostess, are both fresh and fair,
When they give a party no one can compare,
They're ruffling their feathers and preening the wings,
And no one goes home till the fat lady sings.

Refrain:
Tooraloo, tooralay,
And the queen of society lives in Ballae.

Tonight we come swanning to Ballae once more,
Tonight is the last time, there is no encore.
We raise up our voices the message to send,
Like the swans we sing sweetly to signal the end.

Tchaikovsky made swans swimming on a fine lake,
Their costumes like ours were a credible fake,
Their story ends sadly, the birdies did die,
But their spirits immortal will ever more fly.

And where are the swans from the opera house stage?
Their gooses were cooked when they reached middle age,
We think of their antics, their rhymes and refrains,
And remember the days when our swans were young swains.

The curtain must fall and our revels will end,
We'll go down the Swanee and swing round the bend,
Our swansong contains both the smile and the tear,
So goodbye Father Time and hello the New Year!

If Cooks Could Kill

Commemorating the regulation forbidding home baked goods at public meetings,
in this case the Women's group at University College Cork

The dangerous women who frequent the college
Are under suspicion because of their knowledge
Of baking, and making a sandwich or two,
As lethal perhaps as a foul witch's brew:
Stirring the pot like the hags of Macbeth
Laden with microbes and harbouring death;
Not using the usual bats and green toads,
But butter and flour and eggs by the loads.
The fairest pavlova, though whiter than white
May tempt salmonella to haunt you tonight,
While strains of e-coli, augmented by clones
Lurk in our brownies and cookies and scones.
Eschew the warm quiche – it is brimming with cheese
Made with bacteria: don't mention please
Such bugs, who make working in dairies quite easy,
Yet equally able to render you queasy.
And even the tiniest past-er-y crumb
Has oils that can cause a stout heart to succumb
The threat of virus, or even listeria,
Is enough to engender a fit of hysteria
Among the fine women like you and like I
Who may be quite peckish, but don't want to die!
Beware of the prawns and the nuts and the meat,
It is better by far to have nothing to eat –
And if you are hungry, go straight to the shelf
Of your own homely kitchen, and make it yourself.

On Joachim's 70th
December 2005

The older I get, the better I was.
Looking back on my past, as often one does,
I've soared through my life as a form of gymnastic,
Physically, mentally, only fantastic!
Athletically able, with body electric
The intellect agile in subjects eclectic.
I could run, I could jump, I could sing, I could dance,
Skilful at friendships, adept at romance.
I could hike I could swim, I could stand on my hands,
On mountains or beaches in various lands,
Making art, making music, with camera or flute
Knowledge and languages gathered en route.
I've sailed in the rain and I've skied in the sun.
Wherever, whenever … always had fun.

To think of it now … I can do all that still.
Some things never change, and I never will.
The race against time, is a race I am winning.
The best I can be, is in fact just beginning.

Immigrants
January 2006

I saw in the surf an awkward stone
Reluctantly pulled from the ocean floor
Embraced, embedded
And finally wedded
To the shifting sand of the newfound shore.

While a band of sea-spawned barnacles
Artfully grown on a feathered raft
Bleached and dried
And slowly died
On the beach, despite their hopeful craft.

A wayward coconut from who knows where
Discovered by chance at the break of day
Washed in and out
As if in doubt
Whether to root, or to float away.

I too am a rider on the waves,
With baggage packed and held in hand
A new arrival
Unsure of survival
Seeking to live in an unknown land.

Animal, vegetable, mineral, and me
None of us certain of what is to be.
Compelled to embark
On our personal ark
Carried by currents and changeable sea.

24

Sandycove Covenant

If there's a God, it's surely here
He hides his face; where mists ascend
In curtained light without an end
And contours blur which once were clear.
The sea-born cloud and rainbow's arc
Modify both light and dark.

In Genesis the waters part, and earth
Is separate as night from day.
But here, where men and goats might play,
Satyrical in moments filled with mirth,
The promised land by turns is wet and dried,
Then distanced once again by rising tide.

The changeling sea which has no fixed abode
Illusively extends its silken reach,
And stealthily might rearrange the beach,
Or with a flourish, airily explode,
The heartlong surge of waves upon the shore,
Turning time and tide to metaphor.

Air, land and water ... where is fire?
Even in the common gull at flight
There is an element which could ignite,
Spilling joyful laughter from its gyre.
A cosmic view from one small place apart,
A beating vision of the human heart.

Offshore Investment
for Arthur

Adventure lies beyond the waves
To fund this escapade he saves ...
Through clever use of stocks and shares,
Navigating bulls and bears.
Marine expenses he can meet ...
A coat of paint, a jib, a cleat ...
Not till, but tiller claims his hand
For bounty lies beyond the land.
No firm to steer; but firmament
To set a course by, heaven sent!
A rising tide will lift his boat
Not currencies, but currents float
His craft through jewel-encrusted froth.
Both winds of change and sails of cloth
Convey him to the farthest reach
Of silver sea and golden beach.

Whither

For Katherine on her 60th, 2007

What next, and whither? ... Never sere
Despite the way it might appear,
My leaves are flakes, of former flags,
Crumbling shapes, of tulle and rags.
Abandoned now the rich displays
Of blood-red youth, and fine arrays;
The blushing petals dropping down,
Discarded like a dated gown.
Returning just a velvet pod –
I seek an undiscovered sod
On which my precious seeds to sow
And watch enchanted flowers grow.

CONILHAC — PLANÉTIES
ᴬ ALARIC 11/2/06

Lavender for Love

April 2008, for Siobhan Sheehy on her marriage to Liam Kelly

As a romantic gift on this magical night
A lily or rose would be perfectly right,
Though lacking perhaps in both nuance and hint ...
Why not a flower, that is also a tint?

A bouquet of lavender warm from the sun,
Deeply enchanting, and fragrant with fun,
Pervasively spicy it scatters the path,
Flavours the kitchen, and perfumes the bath.

It lines the long road which is still to be travelled,
A skein of fine silk that is being unravelled.
Winding its way towards the mauve-distant slope
Through threads of magenta and heliotrope.

Why not a blossom that's redolent, too
Of a subtle and sensual, passionate hue?
Patina of grapes as they blush on the vine,
And crystalline goblets just brimming with wine.

Impressionist violets which bring up the light,
And skyshades which purple the darkening night.
The deep ultraviolets which go unperceived,
Intuitive feelings, intensely believed.

A colour which dwells between being and seeming,
The indigo firmament starry with dreaming,
In sunrise and sunset, expensive above,
Eternal, ethereal, lavender love.

The Owl

With the passage of time I felt foul,
My laughter an ill-repressed how-l,
But gestalt ther-a-py,
To my lock held the key,
In the guise of a wise, horny owl!

Opera Night
2008

The stage is set, the room is heated
Glass in hand, the guests are seated.
With rapt attention to the art
Of prima donna, and men who start
To stretch their tonsils to impress,
The audience – of the Met … no less!
Expansive gestures, busts abundant,
Fulsome praise is not redundant.
Voce vivace, and gathering forces
Interspersed with dainty courses.
A destiny to sip and savour
Before the plot becomes much graver.
Darkening drama with tears and pleas
And just desserts before the cheese.
For body and soul, there's nothing so filling
As lyrical dining and tragical trilling.
So bravo! Bravissimi! Many 'encore'
And warmest of thanks, da tutti, dal cuore!

34

Alannah's Garden of Earthly Delights

This isn't the time when a muse might come visit,
On a dull gloomy day, or then again, is it?

Just thinking of someone inclined to be cheerful,
Might brighten a day that was verging on tearful.

In face of a climate both darker and wetter,
She builds a symbolic new glasshouse – far better

For growing tomatoes and peppers and herbs,
As perfect perhaps as her nouns and her verbs,

Which transform the daily, the dreary, the real
Into new things to see, and new ways to feel.

The highways and byways conceal hidden treasure
Which Alannah discovers and shares with great pleasure.

From life's raw materials making confection,
Like so many seeds growing up to perfection.

The world isn't Eden; it's never just right,
But a life fully lived, is an earthly delight.

Love is for the Birds
Valentine's Day 2010

Now is the time, in the wood, field and sky,
That passion consumes all the creatures who fly.
Singing while winging, the skylark is thrilling,
While deep in the forest the nightingale's trilling.
Billing and cooing, the pigeon and dove
Deep-throated, full-breasted, give vent to their love.
Romantics have always penned verse for the birds
Whose actions and antics speak louder than words.
Moving and shaking, the peacock is yearning
Alight with desire, the phoenix is burning.
With wiggle the wagtail begins his parade.
The rooster will strut and display his cock-ade.
The drake with his swagger is saucy and plucky,
Tonight is the night when the duckie gets lucky.
Lyrebirds strum in the rustling bowers
Hummingbirds hum while they're kissing the flowers.
Birdwatchers too, may be trembling a bit
At the sight of booby or glimpse of a tit ...
The dodo and loon have been fools to their folly,
Their life was real short, but was certainly jolly.
A swan may be beautiful, loyal and true,
But Zeus when he mated with Leda, just flew.
Love-nest for rent, for the price of a song.
The birds show and tell what we knew all along.

38

Anti-ageing Formula

Alone in my armchair, I'm snug by the fire
Not feeling contentment, but sudden desire,
To leap from the cushions and do what I choose,
Defy some conventions and break some taboos.
To hell with the house keeping, tidy décor –
I'm free to leave dresses and coats on the floor.
I'll paint the room crimson, perhaps the whole town,
Lavishly clad in a form fitting gown,
Or try a new hairdo of purple or red,
With cornrows and colourful beads on my head.
I might order caviar, lobster or wine,
A magnum at least of the finest of fine.
Forget the lean salad, the niggardly portions.
I'm happy with womanly ample proportions.
I'll hire a Rolls, for a day or a week
(People will think I am terribly chic)
And when I have savoured each elegant mile
I may keep the chauffeur on hold for a while …
And speaking of travelling, why not a cruise
To tropical sunsets and breathtaking views,
Take every adventure I'm able to get,
See the whole world from Cape Horn to Tibet.
Sing Wagner's Valkyrie while cresting the summit,
(I don't know the words, but can probably hum it).
And when I return I can author a book,
Appear on the telly, promote a new look,
Say what I please and decide who to be,
Finally finding the essence of me.
So put on the warpaint, the lipstick, the cream
And never, no never forget how to dream.

A Thank You to Richard Wood
2010

We were greeted by pink and white roses
Like ladies on slender stalk
Who bowed in the soft gentle breezes
And scented our mid-summer walk.

They presided again at the table
Exquisite though overblown,
We too became roses that evening
Through a magic entirely your own.

Child Time
For Emily

Time will move quite slowly
when you are very young.
It's good that you have tuneful toys
and songs that will be sung.

Impatient to explore the world
You'll take a year to walk.
Eager to express your thoughts,
You'll finally learn to talk.

And then the world will open wide
With games and friends and play
and dolls and books all tumbling through
and filling every day.

Much joy and wonder … just one wish
as time starts rushing past
Hold each moment; treasure it,
and don't grow up too fast.

Memorial seat dedicated with the inscription:

Sit here and rest your weary feet
Your mind and soul
Take in the beauty of Kinsale
So loved by Howard and Mary Alice Simpson
Proud owners of Folly House 1972-1998

Remembering Howard and Mary Alice

The bench which faces the passing tide
Reminds me of another seat
Before a desk piled high with books
Which opened on a life complete.

Or maybe it's the empty stool
Where she once sat among the shelves
Of spice, concocting magic recipes
To help us to surpass ourselves.

Remember the vine leaves on the trays?
Covered with handmade canapés?
The popping sound of fine old cork?
And the best martinis outside of New York?

We were prized, like pearls, from our oyster shells
A cheek to kiss, a hand to shake …
And when they took their leave too soon,
They left us each other in their wake.

The wisdom of the Follies was never in doubt.
Here such lively currents flow and blend,
By the gleaming bank, near the flowered knoll,
And come to rest, beyond World's End.

44

Born in in 1945 in Laurel Hollow, Cold Spring Harbor, Long Island New York, Marcia Seaman attended Friends Academy, Long Island, and graduated from Vassar College with a BA degree and UC Berkeley with an MA in 1967. She married Gerry Wrixon in Berkeley in 1968 and they have three children, Robert, Adrian and Allie. She moved to Ireland in 1975 and has lived in Sandycove, Kinsale since 1990.

Marcia's joyful and energetic spirit both celebrates and enhances the good in life: her love for literature is complemented by a gift for rendering in her own rhyme; the visual arts she so enjoys are echoed in watercolours from her own hand; she delights in fine dining whether in an eatery or expertly homespun.

She lavishes attention and love on her dependents; three dogs, a horse, a professor emeritus and a donkey.

A.W.